D1823524

Silent Whispers

Lialana Luna

Original title:
Silent Whispers

Copyright © 2023 Loomevalgus OÜ
All rights reserved.

Author: Lialana Luna
Editor: Taimi Karing
ISBN 978-9916-725-70-2

Echoes of Wisdom

Once upon a time, in a village nestled amidst towering mountains, there lived an old sage renowned for his wisdom. The villagers revered him and sought his guidance whenever they faced challenges or dilemmas in life. One day, a young man approached the sage, troubled by the clamor and confusion that enveloped his mind. "Wisest of sages," he pleaded, "how can I find peace within the chaos of life?" The old sage smiled and handed the young man a small wooden flute. "Listen carefully," he said, "for within the echoes of this flute lies the answer you seek." The young man took the flute, blowing into it gently. Instead of music, he heard the soothing sound of silence resonating in his ears. As he continued to listen, the chaotic thoughts within his mind gradually faded away, leaving behind a profound stillness. From that day forward, he carried the flute with him, using it as a reminder that wisdom often lies not in the noise of the world, but in the echoes of silence.

The Subtle Clues

In the heart of a remote forest, where sunlight filtered through the dense canopy, there lived a group of animals who had lived in harmony for generations. One day, a mysterious illness befell the oldest and wisest among them, leaving him bedridden. Sensing the urgency of the situation, the animals gathered around his bedside, seeking guidance. Weakly, the wise elder whispered, "I have hidden my wisdom in this forest, scattered as subtle clues. Seek them out and piece them together to find the cure." Eager to save their beloved elder, the animals embarked on a journey. Patiently, they observed the patterns of nature, deciphered the hidden messages in the rustling leaves, and unravelled the secrets encrypted in the vibrant colors of flowers. Slowly but surely, they discovered the wisdom woven into every corner of the forest. In the end, they found the cure and nursed their elder back to health. From that day forth, the animals realized that wisdom lies not only in the words of the wise, but also in the subtle clues embedded within the majesty of the world.

Myriad Whispers

In the bustling heart of a metropolis, where buildings stretched toward the heavens, a young woman named Maya found herself lost and adrift amidst the chaos. Faced with a myriad of choices and the constant clamor of opinions, she yearned for clarity and direction. One day, she stumbled upon a quiet park nestled amidst the concrete jungle. As she sat on a bench, contemplating her path, she noticed an array of colorful wind chimes hanging from the trees. With each gentle breeze, the chimes began to dance, filling the air with a symphony of whispers. Mesmerized, Maya closed her eyes and listened. She heard the whispers of the wind, carrying ancient wisdom from distant lands, and the whispers of laughter, echoing the joy of children at play. In those whispers, Maya found solace and guidance. From that day forward, whenever Maya felt lost, she sought the whispers in the wind, knowing that within them lay the answers she sought.

The Language of the Soul

In a small village, hidden amidst rolling hills and gentle streams, there lived a young boy named Kai. Since his early childhood, Kai possessed a remarkable gift: the ability to understand the language of animals. The villagers marveled at his unique talent, seeking his assistance whenever they encountered injured or lost creatures. One day, an elderly woman approached Kai, tears streaming down her face. "Dear Kai," she pleaded, "my injured horse refuses all attempts at healing. Can you help?" Kai nodded and approached the ailing horse. He closed his eyes and listened intently to its silent cries. Slowly, the boy started to hum a gentle melody, letting the horse feel the vibrations of his soul. Miraculously, the horse calmed, its wounds healing under Kai's soothing presence. Word of the boy's gift spread, and soon the villagers began to realize that Kai possessed not only the ability to understand animals but also to touch their souls. From that day forward, the village embraced the notion that the language of the soul is a powerful force, capable of healing wounds unseen and forging connections beyond words or understanding.

The Unspoken Truth

In a small village nestled at the foot of a majestic mountain, there lived an elderly woman named Eliza. She possessed a profound wisdom and was known for her ability to see beyond the surface of things.

One day, a young traveler arrived in the village seeking answers to life's deepest mysteries. Hearing about Eliza, he sought her out and humbly asked for her guidance.

Eliza smiled warmly and led him to a serene garden filled with blooming flowers. They sat next to a pond where koi fish gracefully glided through the water.

The young traveler eagerly poured out his questions, hoping for profound insights. But to his surprise, Eliza remained silent. The minutes passed, and the young traveler grew increasingly anxious.

After what felt like an eternity, Eliza finally spoke. "Sometimes, the truth lies not in spoken words, but in the silence between them," she said gently.

With that, the young traveler realized the power of the unspoken truth and found solace in the silence.

The Serenity of Silence

In a bustling city filled with noise and chaos, there lived a wise old man named Samuel. Samuel had spent his entire life seeking serenity amidst the clamor.

One day, a troubled young woman approached him, seeking guidance on how to find peace in the midst of her turbulent life. Samuel smiled kindly and took her to a tranquil park.

They sat on a park bench, surrounded by the symphony of birds chirping and leaves rustling in the wind. The young woman impatiently waited for Samuel to speak, but he remained serene, lost in the beauty of the moment.

After a while, the young woman grew restless and asked, "Why don't you say anything? Don't you have any wisdom to share?"

Samuel glanced at her and replied, "Sometimes, true wisdom lies not in words, but in the serene silence that surrounds us. Listen to the tranquility around you, and you will find the answers you seek."

With those words, the young woman closed her eyes and finally understood the serenity of silence.

Invisible Words

In a small village, there lived a renowned storyteller named Amelia. She possessed a rare gift - the ability to weave magical tales that captivated the hearts of all who listened.

One day, a young boy approached her, curious to know the secret behind her enchanting stories. Amelia smiled and asked him to meet her at dawn near a babbling brook.

As the first rays of sunlight painted the sky, Amelia sat beside the boy, gazing at the dancing ripples in the brook. The boy eagerly awaited her words, but she remained silent.

Puzzled, the boy asked, "Why aren't you speaking, Amelia?"

Amelia nodded towards the brook and said, "The most beautiful stories are often the ones left unspoken. They reside between the words, carried by the wind, and whispered by the heart. Close your eyes, young one, and listen with your soul."

In that moment, the boy understood that the true essence of a story lies not in the words, but in the spaces between them. He learned to tell stories that touched the hearts of others in ways that no words could express.

The Silent Mentor

In a humble monastery atop a serene mountain, there lived an ascetic monk named Hiroshi. He was known not for his words, but for his profound wisdom and ability to guide lost souls towards self-discovery.

One day, a troubled young man climbed the mountain seeking Hiroshi's counsel. The young man poured out his heart, desperately seeking answers to his inner turmoil.

Hiroshi, sitting in meditation, listened intently without uttering a word. The young man grew frustrated at the monk's silence.

"Why won't you speak?" the young man finally shouted in anguish.

Hiroshi opened his eyes and met the young man's gaze. "In silence, we find the clarity that words often fail to convey," he said softly.

The young man stared at Hiroshi, and in that silence, a profound understanding dawned upon him. He realized that sometimes, the greatest mentor is not the one who speaks endlessly, but the one who guides through the power of silent presence.

The Language of Invisible Bonds

In a small village nestled in the mountains, lived two brothers named Asher and Caleb. The brothers were known for their incomparable bond, like no other in the village. One day, Asher fell severely ill and was bedridden for weeks. Despite their deep connection, Caleb was unable to comfort Asher with words due to his own struggle with speech. However, Asher understood his brother's silent language perfectly.

Every day, Caleb would sit by Asher's side, his mere presence soothing his brother's pain. Caleb would gently hold Asher's hand, and in that touch, they communicated all they couldn't say. The bond between them transcended the need for words. Asher found solace in Caleb's unconditional love, knowing that his brother's heart spoke volumes, even without uttering a single word.

In the end, Asher's illness took him away, but the memory of their invisible bonds remained engrained in the village's collective memory. From that day forward, people learned that language could go beyond words, and the silent connection Asher and Caleb shared became a symbol of love and understanding, teaching others to look beyond spoken language and embrace the language of invisible bonds.

The Unspoken Agreement

In a bustling city, two merchants named Isaac and Nathan embarked on a journey to a faraway land to trade their goods. As they traveled through treacherous terrain, they encountered a deep, raging river blocking their path. The only way across was a narrow bridge made of fragile ropes and fraying planks.

Isaac, known for his cautious nature, hesitated to step onto the bridge. Nathan, on the other hand, possessed a daring spirit. Without a word, Nathan crossed the bridge, demonstrating its stability. Isaac observed Nathan's actions and, without a spoken agreement, followed suit, entrusting his life to the bridge.

Together, Isaac and Nathan reached the other side safely, awe-struck by their unspoken agreement and the power of trust. They realized that sometimes, words were unnecessary when actions could speak louder. From that day forward, whenever they faced challenges in their journeys, they relied on their unspoken agreement, knowing that the bond they shared transcended verbal communication.

Silent Harmonies

In a serene village nestled amidst lush meadows, a young musician named Lily aspired to captivate the world with her enchanting melodies. Every day, she practiced her craft, wandering through the fields, listening to the symphony of nature and drawing inspiration from its silent harmonies.

One day, while walking through the village, Lily chanced upon a deaf child named Emily. Curiosity sparked within Lily as she observed Emily closely. Despite her inability to hear music, Emily's eyes danced with joy whenever she saw Lily's violin.

Driven by a desire to share her passion, Lily decided to play her violin for Emily. She played with all her heart, pouring her emotions into each stroke of the bow. As the music filled the air, Emily's eyes shone with delight, feeling the vibrations and witnessing the joy on Lily's face.

In that moment, Lily realized that music had a language of its own, capable of transcending auditory boundaries. She understood that true harmony could be experienced not only through sound but through the connection of souls.

The Mystery in Silence

In a monastery nestled high in the mountains, lived a wise old monk named Master Wei. Known for his profound wisdom, he guided his disciples on the path to enlightenment. One day, a young disciple named Kai approached Master Wei, seeking answers to the mysteries that plagued his mind.

Expecting an insightful discourse of words from his master, Kai was surprised when Master Wei remained silent. Puzzled, Kai waited patiently for a response that never came, until he grew frustrated and questioned the master's silence.

Master Wei smiled and gestured to a nearby garden. Together, they sat in silence, observing the beauty of nature. The rustling leaves, the chirping birds, and the flowing stream painted a picture of serenity. At that moment of shared silence, Kai felt a deep connection to the universe, the answers he sought revealing themselves in the tranquility of the present moment.

From that day forward, Kai understood that sometimes, the greatest mysteries could only be unraveled through rapturous silence. The absence of words allowed space for contemplation, finding solace in the mysteries that whispered softly to his soul.

The Ripples of Silence

In a small village surrounded by mountains, there lived a wise old man renowned for his silent demeanor. Many sought his counsel, and he would listen attentively to their problems without uttering a single word. People marveled at his ability to bring about clarity and resolution without saying a single word.

One day, a young villager approached the old man in distress. He had been in a heated argument with his neighbor and couldn't find a way to resolve the conflict. The wise old man nodded and motioned the young man to follow him.

They walked in silence towards a nearby lake, and once they reached its tranquil shores, the old man picked up a stone and tossed it into the water. As the ripples expanded, he turned to the young man and smiled.

The young man stood puzzled for a moment but then realized the profound lesson the old man had silently conveyed. Without a word, the wise old man had shown him that his actions, like the ripples, could ripple outwards and affect those around him. From that day on, the young man learned the power of his silence and how it could create harmony in his interactions, just like the ripples on the lake.

The Voice in the Void

In a bustling city filled with noise and commotion, there was a lonely man named Samuel. He lived in a small apartment, surrounded by the sound of voices echoing from the walls of the neighboring buildings. Samuel had lost his voice long ago, leaving him in a world of silence.

Feeling disconnected and invisible, Samuel ventured into the nearby park, hoping to find solace amidst nature's embrace. As he sat under a tree, gazing at the bustling world before him, he noticed a small bird chirping melodiously. Although he couldn't hear the bird's song, he could see the joy it brought to others passing by.

As Samuel observed, he realized that even in his silence, he possessed a voice that could be heard in small acts of kindness and gestures of love. Although his words may not be audible, his actions had the power to touch the hearts of those around him, just like the bird's song.

From that day on, Samuel embraced his voice in the void, making a difference in the lives of others even without uttering a single word.

Silent Footprints

In a remote village nestled at the foot of a mighty mountain, there lived a wise old woman named Mei Ling. She was known for her serene presence and ability to find peace in silence. Mei Ling believed that silence could be a roadmap to understanding ourselves and others.

One day, a young traveler came seeking Mei Ling's wisdom. He wanted to understand the complexity of life and find his purpose. Mei Ling, without saying a word, led the young traveler on a journey up the mountain. Together, their footsteps left imprints on the untouched snow.

Finally, when they reached a breathtaking viewpoint, Mei Ling pointed at the footprints they had left behind in the snow. The young traveler was puzzled, not understanding the significance of those silent footprints.

Mei Ling gently smiled and said, "Just like the footprints we leave behind in the snow, our words and actions shape the world around us. Sometimes, it is in moments of silence that we truly understand the impact our lives can have on others."

From that moment, the young traveler discovered the importance of thoughtful speech and silent contemplation, knowing that even in silence, he could leave a lasting impression.

The Silence of Understanding

In a bustling city of diversity, there lived two men named Malik and Daniel. Malik came from a different culture and spoke a language unfamiliar to Daniel. Despite their inability to communicate through words, they became good friends, often sharing a bench in the local park.

One day, Malik began to teach Daniel the basics of his language, and soon they developed a simple yet profound way of conversing. By using gestures, body language, and facial expressions, they could express their thoughts and feelings without using any words.

Through this unique silent conversation, they discovered a deeper level of understanding. Without the constraints of language, they learned to truly listen to one another and embrace the silence between them.

Their friendship became a testament to the power of empathy and the realization that words are not always necessary to convey meaning and create connections. In the silence of their understanding, Malik and Daniel found a language beyond words - a language bound by heart and soul.

The Language of Stillness

Once in a bustling town, there lived a young apprentice who was eager to learn the ways of wisdom. He sought out the famed master who was said to possess great knowledge and enlightenment. The apprentice arrived at the master's humble dwelling and was surprised to find a serene and still atmosphere. The master sat cross-legged, eyes closed, in deep meditation.

Days and nights went by, but the master did not utter a single word. The apprentice grew impatient, longing for wisdom that seemed just out of reach. One day, unable to contain his frustration, the apprentice asked, 'Master, how can I learn if you do not speak?'

The master opened his eyes and smiled, 'Young one, the language of stillness is far more powerful than any spoken word. In silence, truths are revealed and understanding blossoms. Observe the world around you, listen to the whispers of nature and your own heart. Only then will you truly learn.'

From that day forward, the apprentice embraced silence with newfound reverence. He learned to speak less and listen more. In the depths of silence, he discovered a vast reservoir of wisdom that no words could ever encompass.

Whispers of Insight

In a small village nestled among towering mountains, there lived a wise old woman named Mei. She possessed an uncanny ability to hear the whispers of insight that echoed through the winds. The villagers sought her advice, and she would interpret these whispers to guide them through their trials and tribulations.

One day, a young man named Li came to Mei, troubled by a decision he had to make. 'Wise Mei,' he began, 'I hear no whispers of insight. How can I proceed without guidance?'

Mei smiled kindly and replied, 'Li, in the chaos of life, the whispers can be drowned out by our own worries and desires. Still your mind and open your heart. Listen not with your ears but with your soul. The whispers are always there, waiting to be heard.'

Li followed Mei's advice and spent time alone in nature, silent and observant. Gradually, he began to perceive the faint whispers of insight. With each passing day, they grew stronger and clearer. Li discovered that the answers he sought were within him all along, a part of the great tapestry of wisdom that surrounds us all.

The Silent Sage

Long ago, in a distant land, there lived a revered sage renowned for his profound knowledge and spiritual insights. People from far and wide sought his counsel, eager to bask in the light of his wisdom. Yet, despite his fame, the sage rarely spoke more than a few words at a time.

One day, a curious traveler approached the sage and asked, 'Why do you remain silent, while others can't stop talking?'

The sage smiled warmly and replied, 'My dear traveler, words are like leaves in the wind, fleeting and transient. Silence, however, is an ocean of depth and stillness. In silence, I can hear the echoes of existence and perceive the truths that elude most.'

Amazed by the sage's explanation, the traveler vowed to practice the art of silence. Inspired by the sage's presence, he learned to listen attentively, to observe keenly, and to communicate through the profound language of silence. From that moment on, the traveler's life transformed, as he discovered the power of silence in understanding himself and the world around him.

The Secrets of Silence

In ancient times, there was a secluded monastery nestled in the mountains. The monks who resided there were known to possess great wisdom and tranquility. People came from distant lands, seeking enlightenment and hoping to learn the secrets of silence.

One day, a young scholar arrived at the monastery, eager to uncover the mysteries that lay within. He approached the head monk with a flurry of questions, his mind brimming with intellectual curiosity.

The head monk led him to a serene garden filled with blooming flowers and gently running streams. They sat down beneath a blossoming cherry tree, and the scholar began his barrage of inquiries.

Smiling kindly, the head monk placed a finger on his lips and said, 'We shall communicate in a language beyond words, a symphony of stillness.'

And so, they sat in silence, surrounded by the beauty of nature. Hours turned into days, days into weeks, and weeks into months.

Through the contemplative stillness, the young scholar gradually understood that the true secrets of silence cannot be comprehended through intellect alone. They unfurl within the spaces between thoughts, in the vast expanse of the present moment.

Leaving the monastery, the scholar carried this newfound understanding with him. He learned to embrace silence not as emptiness, but as a gateway to profound insights and inner peace. And in sharing the wisdom he attained, he lit a flicker of enlightenment in the hearts of others, for the secrets of silence are meant to be explored and shared.

Listening to the Unspoken

Once upon a time, in a small village nestled amidst rolling hills, there lived a wise old man revered for his ability to listen deeply. The villagers sought his counsel whenever they faced challenges or sought answers. One day, a young woman approached him and shared her heartache. She had been arguing with her beloved and felt unheard.

The old man smiled gently and handed her a small flower. 'Observe this flower,' he said. 'What do you notice?' The woman studied the delicate petals, the vibrant colors, and the intricate patterns. 'It is stunning,' she replied. The old man nodded, saying, 'Now close your eyes and listen to its unspoken language, the message it conveys to your heart.'

As the woman closed her eyes with the flower in her hands, she noticed a slight fragrance, a whispered wisdom that transcended words. Suddenly, she realized the essence of listening to the unspoken, of understanding beyond the surface. She apologized to her beloved, not with words, but with her heart. And their love blossomed once more after truly listening to the unspoken yearnings that lay within their souls.

The Silent Oracle

In a bustling city filled with noise and chaos, there stood a magnificent statue known as the Silent Oracle. It was said that those who approached the statue with pure intentions could receive guidance from the divine wisdom it held. Many sought its counsel, but only a few truly understood its power.

One day, a troubled merchant arrived at the statue seeking advice. He had faced numerous setbacks and felt lost in his pursuit of success. He stood before the Silent Oracle and poured his heart out, expecting a miraculous answer. However, the statue remained stoic, offering no immediate response.

Days turned into weeks, and the merchant continued his visits, frustrated by the Silent Oracle's silence. Yet, deep down, he felt a silent urging to reflect on his own actions. In the stillness of the night, he questioned his motivations, his relentless pursuit of wealth at the expense of everything else.

Finally, in a moment of clarity, the merchant realized that the true power of the Silent Oracle lay in the silent reflection it inspired within oneself. It was not about receiving immediate answers but rather understanding the importance of introspection. With newfound wisdom, he transformed his approach to business, focusing on integrity and compassion. Slowly but steadily, his fortunes changed, and he became not only successful but also respected and loved by those around him.

The Power of Silent Reflection

In a peaceful monastery nestled in the mountains, there lived a wise monk known for his deep contemplative practices. People from far and wide sought his guidance, hoping to find solace and answers to life's perplexing questions. One day, a troubled young woman embarked on a journey to meet him.

When she arrived, the monk welcomed her with a warm smile and led her to a tranquil garden. 'Sit here and observe,' he said softly. 'Watch the ripples on the calm surface of the pond.' As the young woman sat in silence, she observed her own reflection blending with the gentle movements of the water.

Days turned into weeks, and the young woman continued to visit the garden, embracing the power of silent reflection. In the peaceful sanctuary of her own mind, she discovered answers to her deepest questions. The monk guided her gently, reminding her that the answers lie within her, waiting to be discovered.

Through the power of silent reflection, the young woman emerged transformed, embodying a deep sense of inner knowing and self-awareness. She returned to her community, sharing her newfound wisdom, and became a beacon of inspiration for others to embark on their own journeys of silent reflection.

Whispers of the Heart

Once, in a bustling city, there lived a young man who was always searching for answers. He sought advice from others, believing they held the keys to his happiness. One day, while wandering through a quiet park, he noticed a bench inscribed with the words, 'Listen to the whispers of your heart.'

Intrigued by the message, the young man sat on the bench and closed his eyes. At first, all he heard was the noise of the city, but as he focused on his breath, a subtle melody emerged—a whisper from the depths of his heart.

The young man embarked on a journey of self-discovery, learning to quiet the noise around him and listen attentively to the whispers of his heart. He realized that the external world could offer guidance, but true wisdom resided within him. Through this newfound connection with his inner voice, he made decisions aligned with his authentic self, leading to a life filled with purpose and contentment.

From that day forward, the young man became an advocate for listening to the whispers of the heart, inspiring others to embark on their own journeys of self-reflection and discovering the profound guidance that lies within.

The Weight of Silent Words

Once upon a time, in a small village, there lived a young woman named Lily. Lily had a peculiar gift - she could communicate without uttering a single word. People marveled at her ability, and she often found solace in her silent world.

One day, a renowned poet visited the village and heard about Lily's unique talent. Intrigued, he approached her and challenged her to a silent communication contest. Lily agreed, curious to test her abilities against someone who possessed such verbal eloquence.

The contest began, and both participants engaged in a battle of unspoken words. The poet recited vivid verses, painting scenes with his speech, while Lily conjured emotions, using only her expressive eyes and gentle gestures.

As the contest progressed, the villagers marveled at the power of silence. They realized that sometimes, words can be superficial, while silent communication can carry deeper meanings. They began to understand the weight of unspoken words, the ability to convey emotions without the limitations of language.

In the end, the poet conceded defeat, realizing that Lily's silent words had touched the hearts of the villagers in a way his spoken words never could. From that day forward, the village embraced the art of silent communication, appreciating the power it held in bringing people closer together.

The Art of Absence

In a bustling city, there lived a famous artist named Vincent. Known for his vibrant paintings and lively sculptures, Vincent was adored by art enthusiasts from all around the world. However, amidst the clamor of success, Vincent found himself longing for something more.

One day, he decided to embark on a journey to the countryside, seeking inspiration away from the chaos of the city. He settled in a tranquil village, surrounded by serene landscapes and gently flowing rivers.

Vincent soon discovered a small hill overlooking the village, a place where he could be alone with his thoughts. With his easel and brushes, he began to paint the beautiful scenery before him. But one day, out of curiosity, he left the canvas blank, not painting anything at all.

To his surprise, this absence of art spoke louder than his previous works ever could. The absence allowed viewers to interpret their own emotions and project their imagination onto the blank canvas. This absence became the art itself.

Vincent realized that sometimes, emptiness and absence hold a deeper power than the abundance of creation. From then on, he incorporated empty spaces into his paintings, allowing the viewer to complete the artwork with their own thoughts, feelings, and experiences.

In Silent Reverie

In a quaint village nestled deep within the mountains, there existed a wise old man named Kazuki. Kazuki was known for his serene presence and profound wisdom, which he gained through years of meditation and introspection.

One day, a troubled young man sought Kazuki's counsel. The young man confided in him, sharing his worries, fears, and anxieties. Kazuki listened attentively but responded with silence.

Days turned into weeks as the young man visited Kazuki, pouring out his heart and seeking answers. Each time, Kazuki remained silent, his eyes filled with understanding and peace.

Eventually, the young man realized that the answers he sought were not in Kazuki's words but in the silence between them. In the silent reverie they shared, the young man found solace and clarity.

From that day forward, the young man became a devotee of silence. He learned the art of stillness and the power of contemplation. Through silence, he discovered the answers he sought within himself, and he, too, became a beloved teacher, guiding others on their own path of self-discovery.

The Silent Storyteller

In a time long ago, storytelling was a cherished tradition in a small village. Elders would gather around the fire and weave tales filled with magic, wisdom, and adventure. Yet, there was one storyteller unlike any other. Her name was Amara, and she told stories without uttering a single word.

Amara communicated through graceful movements, expressive gestures, and the twinkle in her eyes. Her stories captivated listeners, transporting them to faraway lands and teaching them powerful lessons without the need for spoken words.

One day, a skeptical traveler arrived in the village and challenged Amara's storytelling ability. He believed that true storytelling required words, and he doubted the power and depth of Amara's silent tales.

Amara accepted the challenge and began her performance. As she danced and mimed, emotions cascaded through her movements, transcending the need for words. The traveler was soon entranced, his doubts crumbling with each passing moment.

When the performance ended, the traveler was moved to tears. He realized that words were not the sole conduit of storytelling; silence, expression, and movement held their own enchanting power. From then on, the traveler became Amara's apprentice, dedicating his life to sharing stories that transcended words, ensuring that the silent storyteller's legacy would continue for generations to come.

The Silent Connection

Once upon a time, in a bustling city, lived a young man named Ethan. Ethan was a compassionate soul who tirelessly worked to help those in need. He spent his days offering a listening ear to people who craved connection, solace, and understanding.

One day, an old man approached Ethan with tears streaming down his weathered face. The old man seemed burdened by an untold story, yet no words escaped his lips. Intrigued, Ethan approached him and gently held his hand, as if trying to bridge the gap between their unspoken emotions.

In this silent connection, Ethan realized that sometimes, words were unnecessary. He understood the profound power of presence, empathy, and holding space for someone's pain. Through his mere touch, Ethan was able to offer solace, and the old man found comfort in the unspoken bond they shared.

From that day forward, Ethan learned the art of silent connection. He mastered the language of presence, lending solace to many souls who were trapped in the labyrinth of their own emotions. Ethan taught the world that sometimes, the deepest connections are forged through silence, where words are replaced by genuine understanding and compassion.

The Art of Listening

In a quaint village nestled among rolling hills, there lived a wise sage named Haruki. The villagers sought Haruki's counsel for his ability to keenly listen before providing guidance.

One day, a young villager named Mei sought Haruki's advice in dealing with her troubled heart. Mei poured her heart out, her words flowing like a river. Haruki listened intently, not only to her words but to the emotions behind them.

After Mei finished speaking, she anxiously awaited Haruki's wisdom. To her surprise, he remained silent for what felt like an eternity. Finally, Haruki spoke softly, 'My dear, the art of listening lies not only in hearing words but in understanding the unspoken. I have heard your pain, felt your struggle, and sensed your confusion. Now, it is time for you to listen to yourself.'

With these words, Haruki guided Mei to find solace within her own heart, to trust her intuition, and to truly listen to the depths of her being. Mei learned that the art of listening is not limited to external voices but blooms from the ability to attune to her own inner voice.

From that day forward, Mei became a skilled listener, both to others' words and the whispers of her soul. With her newfound wisdom, she effortlessly guided others on their own journeys of self-discovery by simply reminding them to listen - not only to the world but to the truths that reside within themselves.

The Whispering Wind

In a remote village, where silence enveloped every corner, a young boy named Kieran sought solace in nature. The village was nestled among majestic mountains, and the wind whispered enchanting secrets through the valley.

Kieran spent his days wandering in the embrace of nature, listening intently to the soft whispers of the wind. He believed that in those whispers lay ancient wisdom, waiting to be discovered.

One day, a weary traveler stumbled upon the village, seeking direction on his journey. Kieran, with his profound connection to the wind, offered guidance without uttering a single word. He beckoned the traveler to close his eyes, inviting him to surrender to the wisdom of the whispering wind.

As the wind caressed their faces, embracing them like an old friend, the traveler felt a sense of clarity. In that stillness, he received the answers he had been searching for.

From that day forward, the traveler carried the teachings of the whispering wind with him. He shared the lessons of silence, reminding others that sometimes, the answers we seek can only be heard when we quiet our minds and attune to the subtle whispers of our surroundings.

Lessons in Quietude

In a bustling city filled with noise and chaos, there lived a Zen master named Hiroshi. Hiroshi had a reputation for his serene presence amidst the clamor of urban existence.

One day, a young apprentice sought Hiroshi's guidance, yearning for his tranquil state of being. Hiroshi invited the apprentice to join him in his daily routine, which began at dawn.

As the city awakened, Hiroshi and the apprentice ventured out, immersed in the cacophony of car horns, conversations, and the incessant hustle. Yet, Hiroshi remained calm, untouched by the chaos surrounding him.

Curious, the apprentice asked Hiroshi how he managed to maintain such serenity amidst the chaos of the city. Hiroshi smiled and whispered, 'My dear apprentice, chaos is merely perception. In quietude lies our true nature, and from this stillness, we can observe the chaos without becoming entangled within it.'

With these words, Hiroshi taught the apprentice the power of quietude. He guided the apprentice to find peace within himself, to retreat to the sanctuary of his own inner stillness amidst the chaos of the external world.

From that day forward, the young apprentice carried the lessons of quietude with him. He navigated the city with ease, his heart rooted in peaceful tranquility, and effortlessly guided others on the path to finding solace in the midst of chaos.

The Language of Whispers

Once upon a time, in a faraway village nestled deep within the mountains, there lived a wise old man named Wei. People from far and wide would seek his counsel, for his words were known to hold great wisdom.

One evening, a young man named Li approached Wei, troubled by the challenges he faced in life. He asked the old man for guidance on how to find his true purpose.

Wei smiled and replied, 'My young friend, the answer lies in the language of whispers.'

Perplexed, Li asked, 'What do you mean, Master Wei?'

The wise old man began to explain. 'In life, there are many distractions, loud noises that cloud our thoughts and drown out our inner voice. But if you learn to listen carefully to the whispers of your heart, you shall find the path that leads you to your true purpose.'

With renewed hope, Li embarked on a journey of self-discovery. He spent days in silence, distancing himself from the noise of the world. As he delved deeper into stillness, he started to uncover the whispers buried within his being.

Through the language of whispers, Li discovered his passion for art. He found joy in creating beauty that spoke to the souls of others. Realizing that his purpose was to inspire, he embraced his newfound calling wholeheartedly.

Word spread of Li's remarkable talent, and soon people from all walks of life found solace and inspiration in his art. He became a beacon of light for those lost in the chaos of the world, teaching them to listen to the language of whispers within their own hearts.

And so, Li's journey of self-discovery transformed not only his own life but also the lives of countless others. This parable reminds us that amidst the noise and distraction of life, it is in the language of whispers that our true purpose can be found.

A Lesson in Silence

In a small village, there lived a young shepherd named Tao. He possessed a rare gift - the ability to calm even the wildest of animals with his gentle presence.

One day, as Tao was herding his sheep, he stumbled upon a magnificent lion trapped in a thorny bush. The lion roared in pain, desperately trying to free itself.

Tao approached the lion calmly, emitting an aura of serenity. He spoke to the lion in hushed tones, soothing its fears. Surprisingly, the lion grew quiet, listening intently to Tao's words of reassurance.

Touched by the shepherd's compassion, the lion ceased its struggle. In that moment, Tao understood the power of silence. He gently plucked the thorns one by one, freeing the lion from captivity.

As a gesture of gratitude, the lion vowed to protect Tao and his flock from harm. In the following years, many predators approached Tao's village, but none dared to attack as long as the lion stood by his side.

Word of the miraculous alliance between Tao and the lion spread far and wide. People traveled from distant lands to witness the harmony that existed between man and beast.

This tale teaches us that sometimes, the greatest lessons can be learned in silence. It is through quiet contemplation and understanding that we forge connections with others, finding harmony in the most unexpected places.

The Silent Journey

In a bustling city filled with noise and chaos, there lived a young woman named Mei. She found solace in the simple pleasures of life and sought to escape the hustle and bustle of the urban jungle.

One day, Mei made a life-changing decision. She embarked on a silent journey to a remote monastery tucked away amidst lush mountains. The serene surroundings offered her a respite from the ceaseless noise of the city.

At the monastery, Mei observed the monks as they went about their daily routine in tranquility. They communicated not with words but with gestures and expressions, understanding one another without the need for verbal communication.

Intrigued by their silent harmony, Mei immersed herself in their way of life. She learned to appreciate the power of silence as a means of connection that transcended language barriers.

Months turned into years, and Mei became a respected member of the monastery. Visitors from far and wide would seek her guidance, for she had mastered the art of understanding others without uttering a word.

Mei's silent journey had taught her that true communication goes beyond mere words. It lies in gestures, expressions, and the unspoken understanding we share with one another.

Upon returning to the city, Mei brought the wisdom she had gathered. Amidst the cacophony of urban life, she taught others the beauty of silence, encouraging them to seek moments of stillness and connection amidst the chaos.

This parable reminds us that in silence, we discover our authentic selves and forge connections that surpass the limitations of language.

The Calm Amidst Chaos

In a bustling town, there lived a humble tea merchant named Zhang. Despite the noise and chaos of the marketplace, Zhang always wore a serene smile on his face.

One day, a curious traveler approached Zhang and inquired, 'How do you remain so calm amidst all this chaos?'

Zhang chuckled softly and replied, 'In the midst of chaos, lies the opportunity to find peace.'

Intrigued, the traveler asked him to explain further.

Zhang poured them some tea and began his tale. 'Long ago, I was a restless soul consumed by the cacophony of the world. Until one day, I stumbled upon a wise old man who taught me the art of finding calm in the storm.'

The traveler listened intently as Zhang continued, 'By focusing on the rhythm of my breath, I learned to anchor myself amidst the chaos. With each inhale and exhale, my mind grew still, unaffected by external disturbances. I realized that peace was not found in the absence of chaos, but in our ability to remain centered within it.'

Inspired by Zhang's words, the traveler decided to stay in the town and learn from the tea merchant. Together, they spread the wisdom of finding calm amidst chaos, teaching others to embrace stillness even in the most turbulent times.

Through their teachings, the town transformed into a haven of peace. People from all walks of life sought solace in the tranquil atmosphere that Zhang had created. The marketplace, once filled with noise and discord, became a place of serenity, where even the busiest minds could find respite.

This parable serves as a gentle reminder that amidst the chaos of life, we possess the power to find inner peace. By cultivating stillness within ourselves, we can become the calming force that transforms turmoil into tranquility.

The Wise Sage's Lesson

Once upon a time, in a small village nestled amongst lush green hills, there lived a wise sage. People from far and wide would seek his guidance, for he possessed great wisdom and insight.

One day, a young woman approached the sage with a troubled heart. She spoke of her endless troubles, her struggles, and her battles with the world. The sage listened patiently, his eyes filled with compassion.

After hearing her tale, the sage smiled and said, 'My dear, there is a way to transcend the limitations of words and find solace in silence.'

Curious, the young woman asked how she could achieve this. The sage replied, 'Close your eyes and embrace the beauty of silence. It is in silence that the true essence of life reveals itself.'

The young woman followed the sage's advice, closing her eyes and immersing herself in silence. As the external noise faded away, she discovered a profound calmness within her being.

In that silence, she found the answers to her questions, the peace she had been searching for, and the strength to face life's challenges with grace and equanimity.

From that day forward, the young woman understood the power of transcending words and embracing silence. She became a beacon of wisdom, helping others find solace and guidance in the depths of their own silence.

The River of Words

In a bustling city, there lived a young poet who possessed a remarkable gift with words. His verses were known to move people's hearts and kindle their emotions, and his fame spread far and wide.

One day, overcome with the desire to create his greatest masterpiece, the poet ventured into the wilderness, deep into the heart of nature. As he sat by the side of a river, he marveled at the gentle flow of water, its rhythm reminiscent of the poetic verses he had crafted.

Inspired, he began to compose a poem, pouring his heart and soul into each word. But no matter how hard he tried, his verses fell short of capturing the beauty and serenity of the river.

Frustrated and disheartened, the poet sought solace in silence. He sat by the river, unable to find the right words to express his experience.

Days turned into weeks, and weeks into months, as the poet embraced the silence. He observed the river, its subtle nuances and infinite expressions. He became one with the flow, feeling its rhythm in his being.

And then, one day, as he sat by the river, attuned to its silent symphony, a deep realization dawned upon him. It wasn't the words that could capture the river's essence; it was the silence between the words.

With newfound understanding, the poet returned to

the city and began composing his masterpiece. His verses now carried the power of silence, the pauses reflecting the rhythm of the river. And when he recited his poem, the audience was left in awe, as they, too, felt the presence of the river in the spaces between the words.

From that day forward, the poet abandoned the pursuit of mere words. He embraced silence as an integral part of his craft, enabling his poetry to touch the deepest recesses of the human soul.

The Whispering Winds

In a peaceful village, nestled amidst gentle rolling hills, there lived a young shepherd. He spent his days tending to his flock, surrounded by the beauty of nature and the songs of birds.

One winter's eve, as the shepherd sought shelter from the biting cold, he stumbled upon an ancient temple hidden deep within a forest. Curiosity piqued, he cautiously stepped inside.

To his surprise, the temple was devoid of any statues or altars. Instead, it stood in tranquility, its walls adorned with intricate carvings depicting the wonders of nature. At the center of the temple, a gentle breeze whispered through the trees, carrying with it the secrets of the universe.

Enthralled by the mystique of the temple, the young shepherd decided to become its guardian. He devoted himself to its care, spending his days in silence, listening to the whispers of the wind.

As the years went by, the shepherd's understanding deepened. He learned that the wind spoke a language far more profound than words. It carried the wisdom of the mountains, the tales of the rivers, and the yearnings of the heart.

In the presence of the temple, the shepherd learned to embrace the power of silence. He no longer sought answers in the noise of the world but found solace in the untamed whispers of the wind.

News of the shepherd's wisdom spread, attracting seekers from all corners of the land. They came, seeking guidance, seeking meaning, seeking solace. And the shepherd, with a smile, would simply urge them to listen to the whispers of the wind, for within its silence lay the secrets of existence.

And so, the shepherd and the temple became synonymous with transcendence, reminding all who visited that in the embrace of silence, one could find the profound beauty of life itself.

In the Company of Silence

Once upon a time, in a small village nestled deep within the mountains, there lived a wise hermit named Landon. Landon's reputation for his sage advice and profound wisdom echoed throughout the land. People from far and wide sought his counsel, hoping to find clarity and guidance for their troubled hearts.

One day, a group of villagers approached Landon with a problem they could not resolve. They were constantly at odds with one another, their words filled with bitterness and anger. The air crackled with tension, and peace seemed like a distant dream.

Seeing their distress, Landon smiled and invited them to sit in his humble abode. He sat with them in silence, embracing the stillness that filled the room. Minutes turned into hours as they sat together, enveloped in the company of silence. No words were spoken, yet something magical transpired in that sacred space.

As the villagers emerged from the hermit's dwelling, a transformation had taken place. The bitterness that once consumed them had dissolved, replaced by understanding and compassion. They realized that the power of silence had the ability to heal wounds and bridge divides.

From that day forward, the villagers committed themselves to silent reflection before engaging in heated discussions. They discovered that by embracing the company of silence, they could find the clarity and serenity necessary to navigate the tumultuous waters of life.

The Enigmatic Whisper

In a distant kingdom, there once lived a young prince named Theodore. Theodore possessed a curious mind and an insatiable hunger for knowledge. His thirst for wisdom led him on a relentless quest to learn the secrets of the universe.

One day, while exploring the vast library within the palace, Theodore stumbled upon a forgotten tome bound in dusty leather. Intrigued, he opened its pages to discover a cryptic message written in an enigmatic whisper.

For days, Theodore pondered the meaning of the whisper, delving deep into his thoughts in search of understanding. He sought the guidance of renowned scholars and philosophers, but none could unravel the mystery hidden within those words.

Frustrated, Theodore found solace in the silence of the palace gardens. As he wandered amidst the flowers and trees, a gentle breeze brushed against his face, carrying with it the faint echo of the enigmatic whisper.

In that moment, Theodore realized that the secret of the whisper lay not in analyzing its words but in embracing the silence from which it emerged. He ceased his relentless quest for answers and learned to be present in the moment, attuning his senses to the subtle messages of the world around him.

From that day forward, Theodore learned that true wisdom often requires listening to the whispers of silence, for it is in the spaces between words that the most profound truths reside.

The Art of Emptiness

In a bustling city, renowned for its vibrant arts scene, there lived a talented sculptor named Amelia. Amelia had mastered the art of creating breathtaking masterpieces, each possessing a vibrant and intricate beauty that left viewers mesmerized. Yet, despite her success, a sense of emptiness plagued her soul.

One day, while walking through the busy streets, Amelia noticed a group of children playing in a simple courtyard. Amazed by the joy and contentment radiating from their innocent faces, she approached them and asked, 'What is the secret to your happiness?'

The children looked at each other and smiled. 'Come, sit with us,' they said. 'Let us show you the art of emptiness.'

Amelia joined the children, and together they sat in silence, their eyes closed, absorbing the sounds of the city. In that moment, Amelia realized that amidst the chaos, there existed a serene stillness—a blank canvas upon which life's true beauty could be painted.

Inspired, Amelia returned to her workshop and embarked on a new artistic journey. She began sculpting minimalistic works, free from excessive detail, embracing the power of emptiness. Her sculptures, though simple in form, held a profound depth that captured the essence of life.

Amelia discovered that sometimes, in creating space for emptiness, one can give birth to true beauty.

The Silent Quill

In a world where words held great power, there lived a skilled calligrapher named Evangeline. Her delicate strokes graced each parchment, bringing stories to life and stirring emotions within hearts. Though her talents garnered admiration, Evangeline craved a deeper connection through her art, a longing beyond the realm of words.

One moonlit night, as Evangeline dipped her quill into the inkwell, a whisper swept through her room. Startled, she paused, listening intently. The whisper urged her to put aside her brushes and embrace the silent quill.

Intrigued, Evangeline picked up a quill bereft of ink and began to create. She moved with grace, allowing the silence to guide her hand. With each stroke, intricate patterns and symbols emerged, transcending the limitations of language.

As she completed her creation, Evangeline marveled at the beauty that had arisen from silence. Her silent quill had painted a masterpiece that spoke straight to the soul, touching hearts in a way words could never achieve.

From that day forward, Evangeline recognized the power of the silent quill. She continued to craft stunning calligraphic pieces but always reserved a space for the silent strokes, to remind herself and others of the profound beauty that can emerge from the absence of words.

Finding Solace in Silence

In a bustling village, there lived a wise old woman who was known for her serene demeanor. Many sought her counsel, hoping to find solace in her words. One day, a troubled young man approached her and asked, 'How can I find peace amidst the chaos of life?' The old woman smiled gently and said, 'My dear, the answer lies not in the clamor of the world, but in the stillness within your own heart.' Intrigued, the young man asked for guidance. The wise woman invited him to sit by a tranquil pond and observe the ripples caused by a skipping stone. She whispered, 'Just as the water finds solace after each disturbance, so too can you find peace by embracing the silence within.' The young man pondered these words and as he sat in silence, he discovered that true solace can be found when one quiets the mind, listens to the whispers of the soul, and embraces the stillness that resides within.

Wisdom from Stillness

In a bustling city, there lived a renowned and revered scholar who was known for his immense knowledge. People traveled from far and wide to seek his wisdom. One day, a curious student approached him and asked, 'Master, how did you acquire such profound knowledge?' The scholar smiled and led the student to his study, which was filled with shelves of books. 'The path to wisdom lies not only in acquiring knowledge, but in the stillness that comes from deep contemplation,' the scholar said. He explained that every day, he would take a few hours to sit in silence, seeking clarity and understanding. 'In the stillness of my mind, the volumes I have read come to life. Wisdom emerges when we pause and allow our thoughts to settle.' The student realized that wisdom cannot be gained through constant stimulation, but through the stillness that allows knowledge to become integrated and meaningful. From that day forward, he too embraced the power of stillness, finding wisdom in the depths of his own being.

The Unheard Advice

In a bustling marketplace, a renowned merchant weaved through the crowds, selling his wares. People admired his success and sought his advice on matters of business and wealth. However, hidden amongst the ordinary vendors, an elderly woman went unnoticed. She possessed great wisdom and insight, but her humble appearance rendered her advice unheard. One day, a persistent young man approached the merchant for guidance. The merchant, preoccupied with his own affairs, dismissed the young man with a few generic words of advice. Disappointed, the young man took a moment to rest by a nearby tree. The elderly woman, observing the encounter, approached him. She shared her pearls of wisdom, offering guidance that surpassed any advice the wealthy merchant could have given. The young man was filled with gratitude and asked why the merchant did not possess such wisdom. The elderly woman replied, 'Wisdom is not determined by wealth or stature, but by the depth of one's character and the ability to listen, truly listen, even to the whispering voices that often go unnoticed.' From that day forward, the young man sought wisdom in unexpected places, understanding that the most valuable advice often comes from the quietest voices.

Silent Echoes

In a serene forest, a young wanderer sought answers to the questions that burdened his soul. He journeyed deep into the woods, hoping to find guidance from the wise old trees. As he wandered, he noticed an eerie silence, as if the forest held its breath. Intrigued, he decided to sit beneath a majestic oak tree and wait for wisdom to emerge. Hours turned into days, and stillness enveloped the forest. Just as the wanderer contemplated giving up, a gentle breeze rustled the leaves, and the trees echoed ancient wisdom. He listened intently, and the silence began to speak. The trees whispered stories of resilience, growth, and the passing of time. In their silent echoes, the wanderer found the answers he sought. He realized that sometimes the greatest wisdom lies not in the noise of the world, but in the quiet whispers of nature. From that day forward, he carried the silent echoes within him, a reminder that profound wisdom can be found in the tranquility that resides in every living thing.

Enlightened Hearts

In a bustling temple, there lived a venerable monk known for his radiant smile and serene presence. People sought his guidance, hoping to attain enlightenment. The monk would often sit in silent meditation, drawing wisdom from the depths of his being. Many wondered how he managed to touch so many hearts with his silent presence. One day, a curious visitor approached the monk and asked, 'How do you bring light to the hearts of so many without speaking a word?' The monk smiled and invited the visitor to sit beside him. Together, they observed a lotus flower blooming in a nearby pond. The visitor exclaimed, 'Look at how its beauty brightens the surroundings without any effort!' The monk nodded and explained that the lotus flower does not strive to radiate light, but simply allows its inner beauty to be expressed. 'Likewise,' the monk whispered, 'enlightened hearts need not speak, for their mere presence illuminates the darkness in others.' The visitor realized that true enlightenment comes not from the words we speak, but from the love and compassion that emanates from our being. Inspired, the visitor left the temple with a heart full of light, ready to touch the lives of others through silent acts of kindness and understanding.

The Echo Within

Once upon a time, in a distant village, there lived a young man named Sam. Known for his gentle nature, he was admired by many. One day, Sam decided to take a journey to a nearby mountain, renowned for its enchanting echo. As he climbed higher, Sam shouted, 'I am kind and peaceful!' To his surprise, the echo replied, 'I am kind and peaceful!' Delighted, Sam continued, 'I am loving and compassionate!' Again, the echo responded, 'I am loving and compassionate!' The echo repeated every word spoken by Sam.

Amazed by this phenomenon, Sam repeated words like 'I am joyful,' 'I am humble,' 'I am generous,' and felt his heart fill with happiness as the echo affirmed his positive qualities. Excitedly, he decided to shout, 'I am angry and bitter!' but the echo replied, 'I am angry and bitter.' Realizing the echo only mirrors his words, Sam understood the power words hold over our lives.

From that day forward, Sam always spoke words of love, kindness, and positivity, for he knew that the echo within our hearts reflects back to us the energy we project. The echo within serves as a reminder to cultivate inner goodness and spread it to the world, as the words we choose shape the reality we create.

Lessons Carried by the Wind

In a small village near a vast forest, there lived a wise old woman named Clara. People from far and wide sought her guidance, for she possessed deep wisdom. Clara observed how the wind carried leaves from the forest and whispered secret messages into the ears of those who listened.

One day, a young man named Thomas approached Clara, seeking answers to his problems. Sensing his restlessness, she gently guided him into the forest. As they walked, the wind rustled through the trees, carrying the stories of nature. 'Listen closely,' Clara said, 'for the wind carries lessons meant just for you.'

Thomas closed his eyes and silenced his mind, allowing the wind to speak to his soul. He heard the wind whisper about resilience and the importance of embracing change, about patience and the beauty of waiting, about surrender and the power of letting go. With each message, Thomas felt lighter and more at peace.

From that day forward, Thomas learned to embrace the lessons carried by the wind. He understood that nature holds within it the wisdom of the universe, waiting to be discovered by those with open hearts and open ears. Inspired by the wind, he journeyed through life with newfound wisdom, sharing the lessons he had learned with all he encountered.

The Silent Trail

Deep in the heart of a mystical forest, there existed a trail known as 'The Silent Trail.' Legends said that those who walked upon it would experience profound insights, but only if they ventured in silence. Many travelers were drawn to the trail, eager to uncover its secrets, yet not all were able to remain silent throughout their journey.

One day, a curious traveler named Maya decided to embark on the Silent Trail. As she stepped onto the path, whispers of wisdom enveloped her senses. Entranced by the mystical ambiance, Maya found it challenging to resist the urge to speak. Yet, she remained steadfast, knowing the immense power of silence.

As Maya walked, she noticed the vibrant beauty of the forest. The tall trees whispered tales of growth, resilience, and interconnectedness. The flowing streams spoke of adaptability and the importance of going with the flow. The chirping birds carried messages of joy and the melody of life's simple pleasures.

In the depths of the forest, Maya reached a clearing where a wise old sage awaited. The sage revealed no secrets but simply smiled. Maya understood that the true wisdom lay not in the spoken word but in the ability to listen and observe.

Leaving 'The Silent Trail,' Maya had gained a profound understanding. She realized that the world is brimming with knowledge, waiting to impart wisdom to those who choose to listen. From that day forward, Maya embraced silence as a path to inner growth, and through silence, she discovered the language of the universe.

The Silent Tapestry

In a bustling city, there resided an elderly weaver named Anna. Renowned for her intricate tapestries, her works lay on display in the city's grand gallery. One day, a traveler named Sophia visited the gallery and marveled at Anna's masterpieces. Each tapestry told a story, capturing emotions and stirring the soul.

Curiosity sparked within Sophia, and she sought an audience with the gifted weaver. Anna graciously welcomed her into her humble studio tucked away from the noise of the city. Sophia gazed at the room filled with rolls of thread, vibrant fabrics, and unfinished tapestries.

'I have noticed something peculiar about your tapestries,' Sophia remarked. 'They seem to be silent, yet they speak volumes.' Anna smiled and replied, 'Indeed, my dear. They hold the stories of those who see beyond the threads and listen to the silent language of art.'

Eager to understand, Sophia observed Anna at work. She saw how the weaver paid attention to the silence between the threads, the pauses that held secrets of beauty. Each stitch added depth and meaning, just as silence allows for reflection and understanding.

Inspired by Anna, Sophia began to unravel her own tapestry of life, giving importance to the silent moments—those gaps that hold the power to transform ordinary days into extraordinary ones. She learned that in the tapestry of life, the threads of silent contemplation weave together to create a masterpiece far beyond words.

From that day forward, Sophia observed the silent tapestry of life, finding beauty in the moments of stillness. She realized that, just like Anna's tapestries, life holds profound stories within its silent spaces, waiting to be discovered by those who have ears to hear and hearts to listen.

The Silent Mirror

In a small village nestled at the foot of a mighty mountain, there stood a mysterious mirror. This mirror was unlike any other, for it held the power to reflect one's true self. Visitors from near and far would gaze into the mirror, hoping to discover their deepest desires and hidden flaws. Yet, whenever someone approached the mirror, it fell silent. The village elders believed that the mirror had chosen to speak only to those who could bear the weight of their own reflection.

Years passed, and many tried to unlock the mirror's secrets, but to no avail. Then, one day, a humble traveler arrived in the village. He had spent his life in pursuit of inner peace and clarity of mind. Intrigued by the tales of the silent mirror, he decided to give it a try.

As the traveler stood before the mirror, he saw his reflection, but there was no sound. He closed his eyes, took a deep breath, and listened with his heart. Suddenly, he heard the whispers of his insecurities and fears, the echoes of his aspirations and dreams, and the quiet voice of his true self.

From that day forward, the traveler became the silent mirror's loyal companion. He dedicated his life to helping others discover the power of inner silence and self-reflection. And so, the mirror's silence was no longer a mystery, but a guiding light for countless souls on their journey towards self-discovery.

The Path of Silence

In a bustling city filled with noise, distractions, and constant demand for attention, lived a wise old sage named Rai. He was known for his ability to find peace amidst chaos and stillness in the midst of noise. People would travel far and wide seeking his guidance on the path to inner tranquility.

One day, a young woman named Maya arrived in the city, overwhelmed by the constant chatter and commotion. She had heard of Rai's wisdom and hoped he could teach her the secret of finding silence within. She sought him out and pleaded for his guidance.

Rai smiled and led Maya to a busy marketplace. They walked amidst the hustle and bustle, the voices of merchants, the clattering of carts, and the ceaseless chatter of the crowd. Maya looked puzzled, wondering if she had misunderstood Rai's intentions.

Suddenly, Rai stopped and pointed to a small flower blooming in the midst of all the noise. He asked Maya to observe the flower and listen carefully. As she did, she noticed that the noise seemed to fade away, and all she could hear was the rhythmic sound of her own breath.

Rai revealed to Maya that true silence does not require the absence of noise but rather the art of listening deeply within. The path of silence is not an escape from the world but an embrace of one's own inner stillness, even amidst the chaos. Maya, having learned this invaluable lesson, embarked on her journey towards inner peace, forever grateful for the wisdom bestowed upon her by the Path of Silence.

Unveiling the Silence

In a distant kingdom, there was a grand library considered the pinnacle of knowledge. It contained countless scrolls, books, and manuscripts on various subjects. Scholars from far and wide frequented the library to seek answers to their questions and expand their understanding.

One day, a young scholar named Alina stumbled upon a forgotten chamber within the library. She was intrigued by the door adorned with a symbol of silence and decided to explore it further. As she opened the door, she found herself in a vast hall filled with numerous statues, each with eyes shut and mouths closed.

Curiosity consumed Alina, and she began to inspect the statues. To her astonishment, she discovered that these statues, when touched, emitted a soothing energy that calmed the restless mind. As Alina wandered through the hall, she noticed an ancient manuscript lying on a pedestal. It described the profound wisdom behind these statues and their connection to unveiling the silence within oneself.

Inspired, Alina decided to study the art of stillness and silence. She devoted years to mastering meditation, contemplation, and introspection. As her understanding deepened, she realized that silence was not just an absence of noise, but a profound state of being. It was the vastness that lies beyond thoughts and words.

Alina shared her newfound wisdom with the world,

inviting others to delve into the realm of silence. The hall of statues became a place of pilgrimage, where seekers of wisdom could learn to unleash the power of silence within themselves, unveiling the hidden treasures of their own souls.

The Silent Companion

In a remote village, a young artist named Emilia embarked on a quest to capture the essence of silence on canvas. Day after day, she painted with great passion, hoping to depict the beauty and depth of silence in her artwork. However, no matter how skilled she became, she found it impossible to convey the profound nature of silence through her brushstrokes.

Emilia's frustration grew until she could no longer paint. Desperate for inspiration, she set off on a journey to find a silent companion who could guide her through this artistic impasse. She traveled far and wide, seeking the wisdom of sages, musicians, and poets, but none could offer her the guidance she sought.

One evening, as Emilia sat by a tranquil lake, she noticed a swan gliding gracefully through the water. Mesmerized, she observed how the swan moved with elegance and poise, yet exuded a serene aura of silence. Inspired by this encounter, Emilia realized that silence was not something to be captured but rather embodied.

Returning to her studio, Emilia abandoned her brushes and palette. Instead, she began to create art by immersing herself in silence. She listened to the whispers of her heart and the melodies of the world around her. Emilia's artwork came alive, vibrant with the energy of silence and depth of introspection.

Word of Emilia's unique artistic approach spread far

and wide. Her artwork became a symbol of the silent companion within, guiding others to discover the power of silence not only in art but in every aspect of life.

Silent Lessons

Once upon a time, in a small village nestled between mountains, there lived an elderly woman named Mei. Mei was known for her wisdom and kind heart, and people often sought her advice when facing difficult decisions.

One day, a young man named Li came to Mei seeking guidance. He was torn between two paths, unsure which one to choose. Mei listened attentively as Li explained his predicament, but she didn't utter a single word.

Confused, Li asked, 'Why are you not saying anything, Mei? I came to you for guidance.'

Mei smiled gently and handed Li two seeds—one large and vibrant, the other small and unremarkable. She pointed to a nearby garden and motioned for Li to plant the seeds.

Li did as instructed, planting the large seed with care and tossing the small one carelessly onto the ground. Weeks passed, and to Li's surprise, the small seed grew into a beautiful flower, while the large seed remained dormant.

Understanding dawned on Li as he realized the silent lesson Mei had taught him. It was not the size or appearance that determined the impact, but the hidden potential within.

From that day on, Li no longer sought answers outside himself. He embraced silence as a teacher, learning to listen to his own inner wisdom and find his path amidst the noise of the world.

Louder Impact

In the bustling city of Metropolis, there lived a hardworking cobbler named Samuel. Samuel's handmade shoes were renowned for their quality, but despite his skill, his business struggled to compete with the larger, flashier shoe stores.

One day, a wealthy merchant noticed Samuel's humble workshop and decided to pay him a visit. Intrigued by the cobbler's dedication, the merchant asked Samuel how he managed to survive in such a competitive market.

Samuel gestured towards a shelf adorned with dozens of shoes—each meticulously crafted and polished. Instead of answering, Samuel picked up a simple, unadorned pair of shoes and handed it to the merchant.

The merchant turned the shoes over in his hands, puzzled. 'Why would you show me these plain shoes? They are without any frills or extravagant design.'

With a knowing smile, Samuel replied, 'These are the shoes I made for those who cannot afford the luxuries of the others. For the poor, these shoes bring comfort and protection. The impact of simplicity can be louder than any embellishment.'

The merchant left Samuel's humble workshop with newfound wisdom. He realized that success was not always measured by grandeur, but by the difference one could make in the lives of others.

The Silent Witness

Deep in the heart of a dense forest, there dwelled an ancient tree named Oakley. Oakley had stood tall for centuries, its branches reaching towards the sky, a silent witness to countless seasons and changes.

One day, a group of young explorers stumbled upon Oakley. They marveled at its size and the wisdom hidden within its rings. Impressed by its grandeur, they asked, 'Oakley, what stories do you hold? What lessons have you learned over the years?'

Oakley remained silent, but a gentle breeze rustled through its leaves, carrying whispers of forgotten tales and countless generations. The explorers sat in awe, their minds filled with the unspoken wisdom that surrounded them.

As they bid farewell to Oakley and continued their journey, the explorers understood the silent witness Oakley had become—a reminder that sometimes the greatest lessons are not found in words, but in observation and reflection.

From that day on, the explorers sought solace in nature, listening to the silent wisdom bestowed upon them by the trees, the rivers, and the mountains.

The Voiceless Guide

In a distant village surrounded by mist-covered mountains, there was a mysterious hermit named Wei. Wei was famed for his ability to guide lost souls through treacherous paths, leading them to safety. However, there was something unique about Wei—he was mute.

One day, a young traveler named Ming arrived in the village. Lost and bewildered, Ming sought Wei's guidance, hoping he could help him find his way home.

Despite his silent demeanor, Wei nodded and set off with Ming into the unknown. As they traversed dangerous terrain and ventured through thick forests, Wei never uttered a single word. He communicated solely through his actions, pointing fingers, and writing messages on leaves with a stick.

Days turned into weeks, and the silence between them grew familiar. Ming learned to listen with his heart and trust in Wei's quiet guidance. In the absence of words, Ming discovered deeper connections—a language of gestures and unspoken understanding.

Finally, after a long and arduous journey, Ming reached his village. Overwhelmed with gratitude, he turned to Wei and embraced him tightly, tears streaming down his face. Wei gave a small, knowing smile before disappearing back into the mist.

Ming realized that sometimes, silence could be the greatest guide of all. In the absence of spoken words, it was his willingness to listen and be present that led him safely home.

Silence Speaks Volumes

In a village by the sea, there lived a young fisherman named Kai. Kai was known not only for his exceptional fishing skills but also for his compassionate nature. He had a unique way of connecting with the ocean and the creatures within it.

One day, as Kai was walking along the shore, he noticed a group of children tormenting a wounded seagull. The poor bird lay helpless, its wings broken and spirit crushed. Kai rushed to its aid, shooing away the children and carefully cradling the injured creature in his hands.

For days, Kai tended to the seagull, nursing it back to health. With each passing day, the seagull's trust in Kai grew, and they formed an unspoken bond—a language beyond words.

When the seagull finally regained its strength, it spread its wings and took flight, soaring high above the ocean. Kai watched in awe as the seagull disappeared into the distant horizon.

The villagers questioned why Kai cared so deeply for a wounded bird, to which he replied, 'Sometimes, silence speaks volumes. In the act of compassion, in the absence of words, love and understanding are conveyed. It is through our actions that we truly communicate.'

From that day on, the villagers learned to speak through their deeds, understanding that silence held the power to touch hearts and inspire change.

Discovering in Silence

Once, in a bustling town, there lived a young lad named Ethan. Filled with curiosity and an insatiable desire to learn, he sought out knowledge from all sources. He consulted wise sages, read countless books, and listened to the stories of experienced individuals. But, despite his endeavors, he felt like something was missing.

One day, a wise old hermit came to town and intrigued Ethan with his enigmatic silence. The hermit was known to spend hours meditating in the hills, completely immersed in stillness. Determined to discover the secret behind the hermit's serenity, Ethan sought him out.

Upon meeting the hermit, Ethan asked, "Why do you choose silence over all other sources of knowledge?" The hermit smiled and replied, "In silence, you encounter the deepest truths and unlock profound understanding. Words can only convey so much, but silence reveals the unspoken essence of life itself."

Ethan, intrigued by the hermit's profound words, decided to embrace silence in his own life. He spent hours each day meditating, allowing his mind to quieten, and his heart to open. In the silence, he discovered a wealth of wisdom that words could never convey.

As time passed, Ethan became a beacon of tranquility and knowledge. People sought his guidance, eager to understand the secret behind his newfound wisdom. Ethan shared his story and encouraged others to explore the power of silence. Through quiet contemplation, they too discovered the profound depths that lie within.

The parable of Ethan reminds us that amidst the noise and chaos of the world, true understanding and wisdom can often be found in the silence within.

The Silent Invitation

In a bustling city filled with endless commotion and distractions, there lived a renowned artist named Lily. Amidst the constant noise, she found solace within the realm of creativity. Every brushstroke on her canvas came alive with vibrancy and emotion, capturing the hearts of all who beheld her art.

One day, as Lily worked on a masterpiece in her crowded studio, a stranger stood silently at the entrance, observing her with keen interest. Curiosity piqued, Lily approached the stranger and asked, "Why do you stand so silently without uttering a word?"

The stranger, with a gentle smile, handed her a piece of paper. Upon reading it, Lily's eyes widened with joy and astonishment. The paper read, "I am an admirer of your art, and I believe that silence holds the key to unlocking greater depths of your creativity."

Intrigued by the silent invitation, Lily pondered upon its meaning. She decided to embrace silence in her artistic process. She declined invitations, withdrew from noisy gatherings, and sought solace in reflection and quietude.

Days turned into weeks, and weeks into months. Within the silence, Lily's creativity began to soar to unimaginable heights. Colors became bolder, emotions became clearer, and her art touched the souls of all who witnessed it.

Lily's newfound silent invitation spread throughout the city, inspiring other artists to explore the power of silence. In the embrace of stillness, they too discovered hidden reservoirs of creativity waiting to be unlocked.

The parable of Lily teaches us that amidst the clamor of the world, silence can be a powerful invitation that leads us to our truest and most extraordinary expressions of creativity.

The Silence Within

In a small village nestled amidst majestic mountains, there lived a curious young girl named Maya. She possessed a radiant spirit and an insatiable thirst for knowledge. Maya had explored countless avenues of learning, but she yearned for a profound understanding that eluded her.

One day, as Maya wandered through the woods, she stumbled upon a serene pond. Enchanted by the tranquil surface, she sat by the water's edge, captivated by its stillness. As she gazed into the depths, a voice from within whispered, "The answers you seek lie within the silence of your own being."

Intrigued, Maya decided to embark on a journey within herself. She retreated to a quiet cave atop the mountains and embraced solitude, dedicating herself to the pursuit of inner stillness and self-discovery.

Days turned into weeks, and weeks turned into months. In the depths of silence, Maya encountered her true essence, untainted by the worldly distractions. Like a lotus blooming from the mud, her understanding blossomed with clarity and wisdom.

Maya returned to her village, radiating peace and insight. People flocked to her, amazed by the transformation they witnessed. Maya shared her story and inspired many to explore the silence within themselves. Through introspection and self-reflection, they too found profound answers to their deepest questions.

The parable of Maya teaches us that amidst the clamor of external knowledge, the truest and most profound understanding can only be discovered by delving into the silence within.

The Quiescent Teacher

In a small village nestled amidst lush green fields, there lived a humble and reserved teacher named Samuel. He possessed a wisdom that surpassed his simple appearance, and his teachings had the power to transform lives.

Samuel's students adored him, eagerly gathering every day to soak in his knowledge. However, as he grew older, Samuel's voice weakened, making it increasingly difficult for him to be understood. Instead of raising his voice or relying on technology, he chose a different path.

One day, Samuel entered his classroom, carrying a huge stack of blank paper. He distributed it among his students, signaling them to remain silent. Confused but intrigued, the students complied.

Samuel began to communicate solely through written words, using gestures and expressions to illustrate his points. As the days passed, the students discovered that the silence between them and their teacher opened new channels of understanding. They listened with their hearts and comprehended with depths that surpassed mere words.

Years turned into decades, and Samuel's silent teachings spread far and wide. Students from neighboring villages flocked to learn from the quiescent teacher. Through silence, Samuel's impact grew even stronger, transcending the limitations of spoken language.

This parable of Samuel teaches us that sometimes, the most powerful lessons are not conveyed through vocal utterances, but through the silence that allows us to truly hear and understand.

The Power of Unspoken Words

Once, in a distant village, there lived a wise old farmer named Lao. Lao was known for his ability to communicate without uttering a single word. People would seek his advice on matters of the heart, the soul, and everything in between.

One day, a young man named Koji approached Lao with a heavy heart. He could not find the right words to express his love to a young woman he had admired from afar. With tears welling up in his eyes, Koji sought Lao's guidance in hopes of finding a solution.

Lao listened intently, his calm eyes penetrating the troubled soul before him. He motioned for Koji to sit next to the river that ran by his humble abode. They sat in silence, the flowing water creating a soothing symphony.

As the minutes turned into hours, Koji began to feel a sense of peace he had never experienced before. Lao's serene presence seemed to heal his wounded heart without uttering a single word. The tranquility of the moment awakened Koji's internal wisdom, and he realized that true love need not rely solely on spoken words.

When Koji finally stood up to leave, his heart filled with newfound confidence. He embraced Lao and thanked him for the transformative experience. From that day forward, Koji approached his love interest with a different energy. Instead of relying on spoken words, he let his actions speak louder. And as fate would have it, his love was reciprocated, blossoming into a lifelong partnership filled with love, understanding, and unwavering support.

The power of unspoken words lies not in the absence of speech but in the way silence allows us to tap into the depths of our hearts. It is in the stillness of silence that our true intentions find their voice, reaching out to touch the souls of others.

When Silence Leads

In the heart of a dense forest, there resided a group of animals who faced a common foe. A hunter roamed the woods, threatening their peaceful existence. One day, as the animals gathered to discuss the growing danger, they realized that it was time to take action.

The wise old owl, known for its ability to see through the darkness, was chosen as their leader. Instead of devising a plan filled with tactics and strategies, the owl surprised everyone with its silence. The animals were perplexed, expecting the owl to provide them with guidance.

Days turned into weeks, and the owl remained silent. The animals grew restless, doubting their decision to choose the owl as their leader. But little did they know, the owl's silence was stirring something within them. It was challenging them to find their own voices, to tap into their own wisdom.

As they grappled with their fear, the animals began to realize that true leadership did not lie in blindly following someone else's plan. It was about finding the strength within themselves to take action, to trust their instincts.

And so, one by one, the animals started to stand up, their newfound courage shining brightly. They devised their own strategies, working together to outsmart the hunter. The once silent forest became a symphony of resilience and determination.

When the hunter ventured into the forest, he was met

not with fear but with an unexpected unity. The animals, led by their inner strength, turned the tide. The hunter, defeated by their collective power, left the forest never to return.

The silence of the owl had led them on a path of self-discovery and empowered them to rise above their fears. Their greatest victory lay not in defeating the hunter, but in the realization that they were capable of leading themselves.

The Wisdom in Silence

In a small village nestled at the foot of a mountain, there was a renowned teacher named Akira. Students traveled from far and wide to learn from his vast knowledge, hoping to unlock the secrets of life.

One day, a curious young student asked, "Teacher, what is the key to wisdom? How does one attain true knowledge?"

Akira gazed at the student, a smile forming at the corners of his lips. He remained silent, and the student's confusion grew. Days turned into weeks, and still, there was no answer.

One morning, Akira led the student to the peak of the mountain, where a magnificent view unfolded before them. They sat in silence, the beauty of nature enveloping their senses. The student, lost in the grandeur, forgot about his question.

As the sun began its descent, Akira finally spoke, "The key to wisdom lies in the ability to listen. When we quiet our minds, we open ourselves to the teachings of the universe. Nature, the ultimate teacher, speaks volumes in its silence."

From that moment on, the student understood the profound wisdom hidden in silence. He learned that true learning is not solely a matter of acquiring knowledge but of attuning oneself to the rhythm of the world. When one embraces silence, the whispers of the universe become audible, guiding them towards enlightenment.

The Silent Path

In a bustling city, filled with noise and chaos, there once lived a monk named Zenji. Known for his peaceful demeanor, Zenji sought solace in the simplicity of a silent path that led to enlightenment.

One day, a troubled young woman named Mei crossed paths with Zenji. Her mind was clouded with worries, her heart heavy with sorrow. Intrigued by Zenji's calm presence, Mei approached him with a longing for peace.

Zenji listened attentively as Mei poured out her troubles, her words filled with pain and confusion. But instead of offering a solution, he motioned for her to follow him.

They walked through the crowded streets, but Zenji remained silent. Mei, unable to comprehend his intentions, grew frustrated. Why wouldn't he speak?

Finally, they arrived at a serene garden tucked away from the chaos. As Mei stepped through the gate, the noise of the city gradually faded. Calmness washed over her, and she understood the power of Zenji's silence.

They spent the day in the garden, engaging in mindful activities such as tending to the flowers and meditating under the shade of a tree. Mei's troubles seemed distant, replaced by a newfound sense of inner peace.

Before parting ways, Zenji placed a small token in

Mei's hand. It was a wooden pendant engraved with a lotus flower, a symbol of enlightenment. Mei was grateful beyond words.

Years later, Mei became a renowned teacher herself, passing on the wisdom she had gained from Zenji. Whenever her students grew restless, she would guide them to a silent path, knowing that the most profound teachings arise from within.

The silent path, devoid of distractions, is where the whispers of the soul find their voice. It is where we discover the answers we seek, if only we have the courage to walk in silence.

The Power of Hushed Words

Once upon a time, in a peaceful village, there lived an old sage revered for his wisdom. People from far and wide sought his guidance, hoping to attain clarity and insight. One day, a young man approached the sage, desperate for advice on how to handle a heated argument he had with a close friend.

The sage listened intently, then whispered softly, 'Words have the power to heal or harm, to build bridges or burn them. Be mindful of your speech, for hushed words can mend even the deepest wounds.'

Curious, the young man questioned the sage's approach, expecting a more elaborate solution. But the sage simply smiled and said, 'Sometimes, silence is the most powerful response. Let the absence of words create space for understanding to emerge.'

The young man, still skeptical, decided to put the sage's advice to the test. Instead of engaging in a confrontation, he chose to remain silent. Days turned into weeks, and then into months. Slowly, the anger between the friends subsided, replaced by curiosity and longing for resolution.

One day, the once irate friend approached the young man and spoke, 'I have missed our friendship. I am sorry for the hurtful words I said.' And just like that, with a few hushed words and the grace of silence, a deep bond was repaired.

From that day on, the young man learned the profound effect of hushed words. He encouraged others to embrace silence in moments of conflict and witnessed relationships transform. The power of hushed words became a guiding principle for generations in the village, reminding them of the strength of silence in fostering peace and understanding.

The Untold Story

In a bustling city, renowned for its vibrant culture, there lived an elderly storyteller. His tales were sought after by everyone, for they contained lessons of life that resonated deeply within each listener. One evening, as he shared a captivating story, a young girl approached him and whispered, 'Sir, will you tell me the untold story?'

The storyteller smiled, appreciating her curiosity. 'My dear child,' he said, 'the untold story is not one that can be spoken, but one that must be discovered within oneself. It is a journey of introspection and imagination, where each person finds their own meaning and truth.'

Confused, the young girl wondered if the storyteller was teasing her. However, his sincere gaze assured her that he spoke from the depths of his wisdom.

'Let me share a secret,' he whispered. 'Every story I tell holds a piece of the untold story within it. Listen not only with your ears, but also with your heart, and you will uncover the hidden treasures of wisdom.'

From that day on, the young girl listened attentively to the stories, allowing herself to be transported to magical worlds. She discovered that each tale contained a unique message meant only for her. And as she grew older, she realized that the untold story was not just a single narrative but a collection of countless narratives, waiting to be unraveled by those willing to seek the depths of their own souls.

The young girl eventually became a storyteller herself, captivating audiences with her own tales. Whenever someone asked for the untold story, she would smile, understanding that the true power lies not in its telling but in the journey of self-discovery it inspires.

The Soundless Lesson

In a distant mountain monastery, silence was revered as a sacred practice. The monks dedicated themselves to the pursuit of inner peace and enlightenment through meditation and contemplation. One day, a curious young traveler arrived at the monastery seeking guidance in his own chaotic life.

The head monk welcomed the traveler and introduced him to the monastery's practice of silence. 'Silence is not merely the absence of sound,' he explained. 'It is a profound state of being, where one can listen to the whispers of their own heart and the wisdom of the universe.'

Intrigued, the traveler decided to immerse himself in the monastery's routine. Days turned into weeks, and the traveler embraced the tranquility that surrounded him. Surrounded by serene landscapes and the hushed footsteps of the monks, he began to uncover the depths of his own thoughts and emotions.

Months passed, and the traveler felt as though he had discovered a hidden treasure within himself. The soundless lessons taught him patience, compassion, and the profound beauty of stillness. He experienced moments of clarity and understanding, realizing that in the absence of noise, he could hear the gentle whispers of his own soul.

When the time came for the traveler to bid farewell, he thanked the head monk for the invaluable lessons he had learned. 'But how can I continue this practice in the chaos of the outside world?' he asked.

The head monk smiled knowingly and replied, 'Remember, true silence exists within, even amidst the clamor of the world. Cultivate inner stillness amidst the chaos, and you will carry the soundless lesson with you wherever you go.'

Inspired and determined, the traveler embarked on his journey, carrying within him the gift of silence. From that day on, he discovered that even in the bustling city streets, he could find solace and peace by tapping into the soundless lesson he had learned in the monastery.

Sacred Silence

Deep in a hidden forest, there stood an ancient temple known as the Sanctuary of Sacred Silence. People from far and wide sought solace in its hallowed halls, yearning for a refuge from the chaos of the world. Within the temple resided an enlightened monk, quietly devoted to the practices of meditation and self-reflection.

One day, a troubled soul approached the monk, burdened with the weight of their worries. The monk listened with compassion and then led the visitor to the heart of the temple—a sacred chamber known as the Hall of Silence.

Entering the chamber, the visitor felt an otherworldly calmness enveloping their entire being. The walls were adorned with ancient symbols, and the air seemed to vibrate with tranquility. In the center of the chamber, a single candle flickered, providing gentle illumination.

The monk motioned for the visitor to sit in silence. 'In this chamber,' the monk whispered, 'words are unnecessary. Here, you will discover the profound peace that lies beyond the noise and chatter of the mind.'

Days turned into weeks, and the visitor immersed themselves in the sacred silence of the chamber. In the stillness, they experienced moments of clarity and insight, unearthing the answers to their most challenging questions. The burdens that once weighed them down slowly dissipated, replaced by a newfound sense of serenity.

When the day came for the visitor to leave, they thanked the monk for the transformative experience. 'But how can I recreate this sacred silence in my daily life?' they asked.

The monk smiled and uttered, 'Sacred silence resides within you. Seek moments of stillness in your daily routine. Whether it be a walk in the park, observing the moon, or pausing to simply breathe, you can tap into the eternal peace that resides within.'

Determined to carry the essence of sacred silence, the visitor embarked on their journey, knowing that the transformative power of stillness was always within reach.

In the Spaces Between

Once upon a time, in a bustling city, there were two friends named Maya and Liam. They were both musicians, but while Maya loved the vibrant sounds of the city, Liam found solace in the quiet spaces of nature.

One day, Maya invited Liam to join her on stage for a grand concert. Excited, Liam agreed, though a part of him yearned for the tranquility of the woods. As the concert day approached, Maya practiced tirelessly, filling the air with melodies and harmonies.

On the day of the concert, the city's concert hall was a sea of people eagerly waiting to be immersed in Maya's music. As Maya began playing, the crowd applauded enthusiastically. But in the midst of the applause, Liam discovered something magical – the spaces between the notes.

Liam realized that while Maya's music was filled with passion and energy, it was in the moments of silence in between where the true beauty resided. The silence allowed the music to breathe, to stir emotions deep within. Liam longed to share this discovery, but he knew he couldn't interrupt Maya's performance. Instead, he quietly sat back and observed, savoring the hidden melodies carried within the silence.

From that day forward, Liam learned to embrace both the music and the silences. He would often retreat to the woods, where nature's symphony whispered in his ears. And when he returned to the city, he would join Maya on stage, adding his gentle melodies, harmonizing with her vibrant tunes. Together, their music became a symphony of both sound and silence, enchanting all who listened. For it is in the spaces between that we find the whispers of our true selves, and the stories waiting to be heard.

Divine Silence

In a small village nestled between serene hills, there lived a wise old man named Simeon. People from far and wide sought his counsel, knowing that he possessed a deep understanding of life's mysteries.

One day, a troubled young man named Sebastian approached Simeon, burdened by the weight of his restless thoughts. As Sebastian poured his heart out, Simeon listened attentively, his eyes filled with compassion. When Sebastian finally finished speaking, expecting profound words of wisdom, Simeon surprised him with just a single gesture – he pressed his finger to his lips, indicating silence.

Puzzled, Sebastian began to protest, but Simeon gently interrupted him. 'Sometimes, my dear child,' Simeon spoke softly, 'the answers we seek lie not in my words, but in the silence between them. It is in that pause, that emptiness, that we can connect to the divine.'

Sebastian pondered these words and decided to embark on a silent retreat to a nearby monastery, seeking solitude in search of guidance. In the stillness of the monastery, with no words to distract him, Sebastian immersed himself in meditation and introspection.

Days turned into weeks, and weeks into months. The more Sebastian embraced the silence, the more he discovered a profound connection to his inner self. In the absence of words, he found solace and clarity. Through silence, he learned to listen to the quiet whispers of his soul, and the divine guidance that resided within.

When Sebastian returned to the village, his demeanor had changed. He no longer sought answers from others but carried within him the wisdom of the divine silence. People marveled at the transformation and began seeking Sebastian's counsel instead. Sebastian, now a humble guide, would often sit in silence with those in need, knowing that sometimes, the most profound healing words are those left unspoken.

The Silent Compass

Once upon a time, in a bustling seafaring town, there was a renowned captain named Captain Elias. He was known for his bravery and cunning navigation, always leading his crew through dangerous waters to safety.

One foggy morning, as Captain Elias prepared for his next voyage, he discovered that his compass was broken. Without his trusted navigation tool, he was unable to set sail. Frustrated and anxious, he scoured the town for a new compass, but none could be found.

Just as Captain Elias was about to give up hope, a frail and elderly man approached him. The man possessed a peculiar stillness that captured Captain Elias' attention. 'Captain, I have an old compass that belonged to my ancestors,' the man said in a whisper. 'It might be broken, but it still holds a secret.'

Intrigued, Captain Elias accepted the old compass. To his surprise, it did not point north like a typical compass. Instead, it remained in a constant state of stillness, refusing to provide any direction. Confused and disheartened, Captain Elias turned to the old man for an explanation.

The old man smiled and spoke softly, 'Captain, the true navigation lies not in the pointing of a compass, but in the silence within you. The compass simply reminds you to trust the quiet whispers of your instincts, the wisdom that arises when you still your mind.'

Moved by these words, Captain Elias understood the ancient wisdom hidden within the silent compass. He embarked on his voyage, relying not on the direction shown by the compass but on the silent guidance that resided within his heart. As he sailed through treacherous waters, he learned to listen to the subtle currents and the rhythm of the waves, trusting the stillness within him to guide his path.

From that day forward, Captain Elias became known as the captain with the silent compass. He continued to lead his crew through the most perilous voyages, relying on the power of silence to steer them toward their destination. And even in the midst of raging storms, the silent compass within Captain Elias always found its way, reminding him that true navigation lies not in the direction shown, but in the silent depths of his own soul.

The Silent Observer

In a bustling city filled with noise and chaos, there lived a man named Ethan. Amidst the clamor of life, Ethan found solace in observing the world around him. From the busy streets to the quiet parks, he let the world unfold in front of his watchful eyes.

One day, as Ethan sat by a café window, a homeless woman caught his attention. She shuffled along the sidewalk, invisible to most passersby. Intrigued, Ethan took interest in a book the woman carried, her only companion in an unkind world.

Weeks turned into months, and Ethan found himself waiting for the woman every day. Curiosity turned into fascination, and he couldn't resist contemplating how she found solace in her silent routine. One day, he mustered the courage to approach her.

'Excuse me, ma'am,' Ethan said, 'I've noticed you reading that same book for months. Would you mind telling me what you find within its pages?' The woman studied Ethan for a moment before speaking softly, 'This book teaches me to find sanctuary in the silent observation of life. It reminds me that as an observer, I hold the power to see the unseen and hear the unheard.'

Intrigued by her response, Ethan began reading the book. Its pages whispered ancient wisdom, revealing that observation was not just witnessing, but merging with the unspoken stories hidden beneath the surface.

Inspired, Ethan started to immerse himself in the art

of silent observation. He sat in parks and watched children play, witnessing their untamed joy. He looked up at the night sky, connecting with the mysterious dance of stars. Through this silent observation, Ethan noticed the intricate beauty of everyday moments that often went unnoticed by hurried gazes.

As the years passed, Ethan became known as the silent observer. His keen eyes could capture the essence of a moment with a simple glance. People sought him out, wanting to see the world through his perspective, to experience the magic of silent observation. Ethan showed them that by quieting the inner chatter, one could truly see the world and understand its profound interconnectedness. For in the realm of silence, secrets unfold, and the extraordinary reveals itself.